George Frideric
HANDEL

ISRAEL IN EGYPT
HWV 54
(1739)

Vocal Score
Klavierauszug

PETRUCCI LIBRARY PRESS

ISRAEL IN EGYPT

PART I.

RECITATIVE.

Now there arose a new king over Egypt, which knew not Joseph; and he set over Israel taskmasters to afflict them with burthens, and they made them serve with rigour.

burdens.

Ex. i. 8, 11, 13.

CHORUS.

And the children of Israel sighed by reason of the bondage, and their cry came up unto God. They oppressed them with burthens, and made them serve with rigour; and their cry came up unto God.—*Ex.* ii. 23.

RECITATIVE.

Then sent He Moses, His servant, and Aaron whom He had chosen; these shewed His signs among them, and wonders in the land of Ham.

He turned their waters into blood.

Ps. cv. 26, 27, 29.

CHORUS.

They loathed to drink of the river. He turned their waters into blood.

Ex. vii. 18, 19.

AIR.

Their land brought forth frogs, yea even in their king's chambers.

Ps. cv. 30.

He gave their cattle over to the pestilence; blotches and blains broke forth on man and beast.—*Ex.* xi. 9, 10.

CHORUS.

He spake the word, and there came all manner of flies and lice in all their quarters.

He spake; and the locusts came without number, and devoured the fruits of the ground.—*Ps.* cv. 31, 34, 35.

CHORUS.

He gave them hailstones for rain; fire mingled with the hail ran along upon the ground.

Ps. cv. 32; *Ex.* ix. 23, 24.

CHORUS.

He sent a thick darkness over the land, even darkness which might be felt.—*Ex.* x. 21.

CHORUS.

He smote all the first-born of Egypt, the chief of all their strength.

Ps. cv. 36, 37.

CHORUS.

But as for His people, He led them forth like sheep: He brought them out with silver and gold; there was not one feeble person among their tribes.—*Ps.* lxxviii. 53; cv. 37.

CHORUS.

Egypt was glad when they departed, for the fear of them fell upon them.

CHORUS.

He rebuked the Red Sea, and it was dried up.—*Ps.* cvi. 9.

He led them through the deep as through a wilderness.—*Ps.* cvi. 9.

But the waters overwhelmed their enemies, there was not one of them left.—*Ps.* cvi. 11.

CHORUS.

And Israel saw that great work that the Lord did upon the Egyptians; and the people feared the Lord, and believed the Lord and His servant Moses.—*Ex.* xiv. 31.

PART II

CHORUS.

Moses and the children of Israel sung this song unto the Lord, and spake, saying: I will sing unto the Lord, for He hath triumphed gloriously; the horse and his rider hath He thrown into the sea.—*Ex.* xv. 1.

DUET.

The Lord is my strength and my song; He is become my salvation.
Ex. xv. 2.

CHORUS.

He is my God, and I will prepare Him an habitation; my father's God, and I will exalt Him.—*Ex.* xv. 2.

DUET.

The Lord is a man of war: Lord is His name. Pharaoh's chariots and his host hath He cast into the sea; his chosen captains also are drowned in the Red Sea.—*Ex.* xv. 3, 4.

CHORUS.

The depths have covered them: they sank into the bottom as a stone.
Ex. xv. 5.

CHORUS.

Thy right hand, O Lord, is become glorious in power; Thy right hand, O Lord, hath dashed in pieces the enemy.
Ex. xv. 6.

CHORUS.

And in the greatness of Thine excellency Thou hast overthrown them that rose up against Thee.—*Ex.* xv. 7.

CHORUS.

Thou sentest forth Thy wrath, which consumed them as stubble.—*Ex.* xv. 7.

CHORUS.

And with the blast of Thy nostrils the waters were gathered together, the floods stood upright as an heap, and the depths were congealed in the heart of the sea.—*Ex.* xv. 8.

AIR.

The enemy said, I will pursue, I will overtake, I will divide the spoil; my lust shall be satisfied upon them; I will draw my sword, my hand shall destroy them.—*Ex.* xv. 9.

AIR.

Thou didst blow with the wind, the sea covered them; they sank as lead in the mighty waters.—*Ex.* xv. 10.

CHORUS.

Who is like unto Thee, O Lord, among the gods? Who is like Thee, glorious in holiness, fearful in praises, doing wonders?

Thou stretchedst out Thy right hand, the earth swallowed them.
Ex. xv. 11, 12.

DUET.

Thou in Thy mercy hast led forth Thy people which Thou hast redeemed; Thou hast guided them in Thy strength unto Thy holy habitation.—*Ex.* xv. 13.

CHORUS.

The people shall hear, and be afraid: sorrow shall take hold on them: all the inhabitants of Canaan shall melt away: by the greatness of Thy arm they shall be as still as a stone; till Thy people pass over, O Lord, which Thou hast purchased.—*Ex.* xv. 14, 15, 16.

AIR.

Thou shalt bring them in, and plant them in the mountain of Thine inheritance, in the place, O Lord, which Thou hast made for Thee to dwell in, in the Sanctuary, O Lord, which Thy hands have established.—*Ex.* xv. 17.

CHORUS.

The Lord shall reign for ever and ever.—*Ex.* xv. 18.

RECITATIVE.

For the horse of Pharaoh went in with his chariots and with his horsemen into the sea, and the Lord brought again the waters of the sea upon them; but the children of Israel went on dry land in the midst of the sea.—*Ex.* xv. 19.

CHORUS.

The Lord shall reign for ever and ever.—*Ex.* xv. 18.

RECITATIVE.

And Miriam the prophetess, the sister of Aaron, took a timbrel in her hand; and all the women went out after her with timbrels and with dances. And Miriam answered them:
Ex. xv. 20, 21.

SOLO AND CHORUS.

Sing ye to the Lord, for He hath triumphed gloriously; the horse and his rider hath He thrown into the sea.
Ex. xv. 21, 18.

PART I.

PART II.

First performance: April 4, 1739
London: The King's Theatre in the Haymarket
Soli, Chorus and Orchestra / Geroge Frideric Handel

This score is a digitally-enhanced, unabridged reprint of the vocal score first issued by G. Schirmer of New York in 1900 (plate 14900). The size has been slightly modified to fit the present format.

ISRAEL IN EGYPT
HWV 54
PART I
Exodus
Nº 1. RECIT._ "Now there arose."

Charles Jennens

George Frideric Handel

Piano reduction by Felix Mendelssohn
Edited by H.W. Nicholl

Nº 2. DOUBLE CHORUS._ "And the children of Israel."

PETRUCCI LIBRARY PRESS

8

Nº 3. RECITATIVE.— "Then sent He Moses."

Nº 4. CHORUS.— "They loathed to drink."

No 5. AIR. — "Their land brought forth frogs."

No 6. Double Chorus.—"He spake the word."

22

Nº 7. DOUBLE CHORUS. —"He gave them hailstones."

★) another reading gives
the tonic triad here:

Nº 8. CHORUS. — "He sent a thick darkness."

NO 9. CHORUS. —"He smote all the first-born."

44

45

Nº 10. CHORUS.—"But as for His people."

Nº 11. CHORUS. — "Egypt was glad."

Nº 12. DOUBLE CHORUS. — "He rebuked the Red Sea."

Nº 13. DOUBLE CHORUS.— "He led them through the deep."

Nº 14. CHORUS. — "But the waters overwhelmed their enemies."

№ 15. DOUBLE CHORUS. — "And Israel saw."

Nº 16. CHORUS.— "And believed the Lord."

END OF PART

78

PART II.
Moses' Song.

№ 17. DOUBLE CHORUS.—"Moses, and the children of Israel."

Nº 18. DOUBLE CHORUS.—"I will sing unto the Lord."

No. 19. DUET.—"The Lord is my strength."

Nº 20. DOUBLE CHORUS._ "He is my God."

N.º 21. CHORUS.— "And I will exalt him."

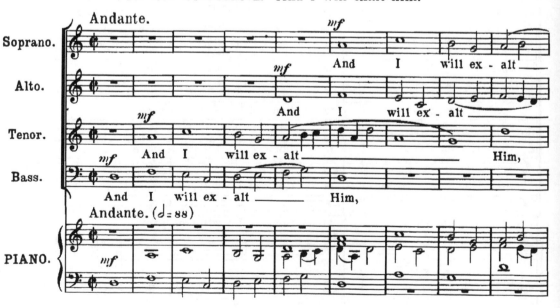

Nọ 22. DUET. — "The Lord is a man of war."

PIANO.

Andante allegro. ($\quad$= 112)

Bass I.

The Lord is a man of

cast

hath ___ He ___ cast ___

in - to the sea.

in - to the sea.

His chosen captains al - so are drowned, al - so are drowned,

His chosen captains al - so are drowned,

drowned in the Red Sea.

drowned in the Red Sea.

Nº 23. DOUBLE CHORUS.— "The depths have cover'd them."

N⁰ 24. Double Chorus. — "Thy right hand, O Lord."

piec-es, hath dash-ed in piec-es the en-e-my.

piec-es, hath dash-ed in piec-es the en-e-my.

piec-es, hath dash-ed in piec-es the en-e-my.

Thy right hand, O Lord, hath dash-ed in

Thy right hand, O Lord, hath dash-ed in

Thy right hand, O Lord, hath dash-ed in

Thy right hand, O Lord, hath dash-ed in

Thy right hand, O Lord, hath dash-ed in

Thy right hand, O

Thy right hand, O

Thy right hand, O

piec-es, hath dash-ed in piec-es the en-e-my, Thy right hand, O

piec-es, hath dash-ed in piec-es the en-e-my, Thy right hand, O Lord,

piec-es, hath dash-ed in piec-es the en-e-my, Thy right hand, O Lord,

piec-es, hath dash-ed in piec-es the en-e-my, Thy right hand, O Lord,

piec-es, hath dash-ed in piec-es the en-e-my, Thy right hand, O Lord,

Nº26. DOUBLE CHORUS. — "Thou sentest forth Thy wrath."

№ 27. CHORUS. —"And with the blast."

No. 28. AIR.—"The enemy said."

Nº 29. AIR.— "Thou didst blow."

lead, they sank as lead, as lead in the mighty wa - - - ters, they sank as lead as lead in the mighty wa - - - ters, they sank, they sank as lead in the might-y wa - - - - - - ters, in the might-y wa - ters: Thou didst

No 30. DOUBLE CHORUS.—"Who is like unto Thee?"

Grave.

prais-es, do-ing won-ders, Thou stretchedst out Thy right hand:

Nọ 31. DOUBLE CHORUS.—"The earth swallowed them."

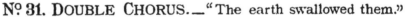

Nº 32. DUET. — "Thou, in Thy mercy."

Nº 33. Double Chorus.— "The people shall hear."

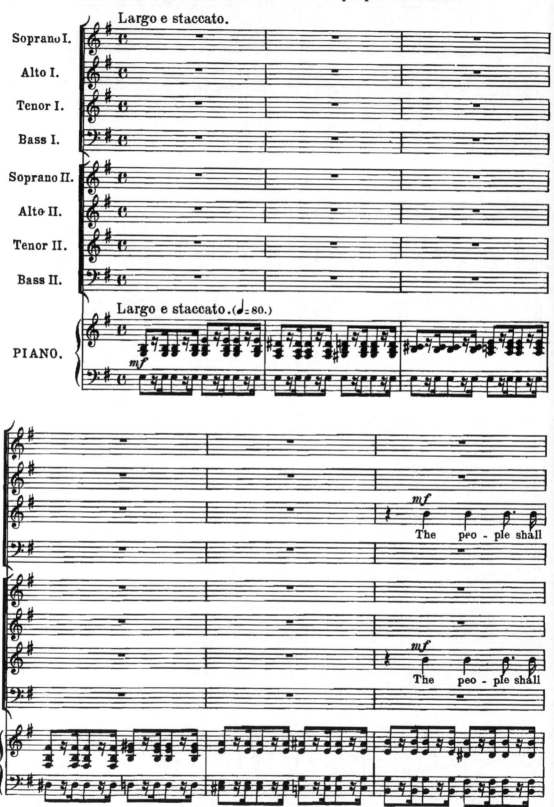

164

172

Nº 34. AIR.— "Thou shalt bring them in."

№35. DOUBLE CHORUS. — "The Lord shall reign."

No. 36. RECIT.—"For the horse of Pharaoh."

Recit.

Tenor.

For the horse of Pha-raoh went in with his chariots and with his

PIANO.

horsemen in-to the sea, and the Lord brought a-gain the wa-ters of the sea up-

on them: but the children of Is-rael went on dry land in the midst of the sea.

No. 37. DOUBLE CHORUS.—"The Lord shall reign."

A tempo giusto.

Soprano I.

Alto I.

The Lord shall reign for ev - er and ev - - -

Tenor I.

The Lord shall reign for ev - er and ev - - -

Bass I.

Soprano II.

Alto II.

The Lord shall reign for ev - er and ev - - -

Tenor II.

The Lord shall reign for ev - er and ev - - -

Bass II.

A tempo giusto. (♩ = 88.)

PIANO.

poco stacc.

No. 38. RECIT. — "And Miriam, the Prophetess".

Tenor.

And Mir-i-am, the pro-phe-tess, the sis-ter of Aa-ron,

PIANO.

took a tim-brel in her hand, and all the wo-men went out af-ter her with

tim-brels and with danc-es, and Mir-iam an-swer-ed them:

N⁰ 39. SOLO and DOUBLE CHORUS. — "Sing ye to the Lord."

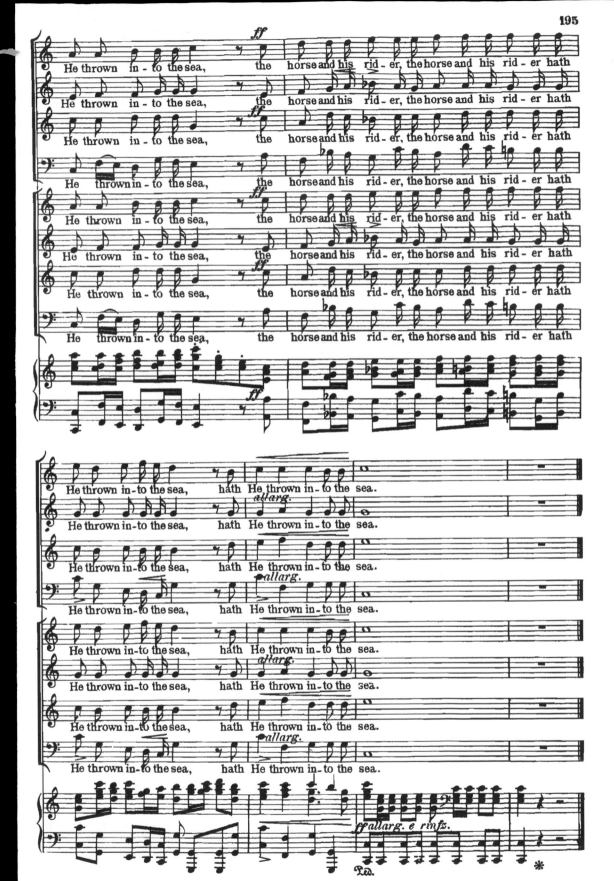

I)

CPSIA information can be obtained
at www.ICGtesting.com
Printed in the USA
FFHW011129110120
57661570-63043FF